almond blossoms

and beyond

almond blossoms and beyond

mahmoud darwish

translated by Mohammad Shaheen

Interlink Books

An imprint of Interlink Publishing Group, Inc.
Northampton, Massachusetts

First published in 2009 by

INTERLINK BOOKS
An imprint of Interlink Publishing Group, Inc.
46 Crosby Street, Northampton, Massachusetts 01060
www.interlinkbooks.com

Originally published in Arabic by Riad El-Rayyes, Beirut, Lebanon

Library of Congress Cataloging-in-Publication Data
Darwish, Mahmud.
[Ka-zahr al-lawz aw ab'ad. English]
Almond blossoms and beyond / by Mahmoud Darwish ; translated by Mohammad Shaheen.
—1st ed.
p. cm.
ISBN 978-1-56656-755-8 (hardback)
I. Shahin, Muhammad. II. Title.
PJ7820.A7K313 2009
892.7'16—dc22

2008055674

Printed and bound in the United States of America

Cover image of almond tree © Bukko/Dreamstime.com

To request our complete 48-page full-color catalog, please call us toll free at 1-800-238-LINK, visit our website at www.interlinkbooks.com or write to:
Interlink Publishing
46 Crosby Street, Northampton, MA 01060
e-mail: info@interlinkbooks.com

Acknowledgments

I have received invaluable detailed comments from Mohammad Asfour, who has read and criticized drafts of these translations, and to Amro Naddy, who worked on earlier versions of some of this material. I particularly thank him for some of the layout suggestions he kindly provided. For her gracious and expert editing and for her patience throughout the project, Pamela Thompson deserves special thanks.

I am indebted to Dina Salman and Ala' Yaghi, graduate students who have assisted with proofreading and made meticulous remarks.

Nabil Matar (a comrade for over four decades) of the University of Minnesota, has been always supportive, and I would like to express my deep appreciation for his enthusiasm and commitment to Darwish's poetry.

I wish to thank Hanin Khirfan, a lecturer in the English department, and Fairouz Bahlaq, a secretary of the Department, who ably typed the material and helped me in the manuscript preparation.

Introduction

Mahmoud Darwish
13 March 1941–9 August 2008

Mahmoud Salem Darwish was born in al-Birwah, a village in the city district of Western Galilee, in Palestine, to a farming family. His father was a moderately well-off farmer; his mother, who could neither read nor write, was the daughter of the headman of the village of al-Damun. Mahmoud was the second of eight children, five sons, and three daughters. After the Zionists occupied, demolished, and drove away the inhabitants of al-Birwah in 1948, the family fled to Lebanon.

> One summer night, I was suddenly woken from sleep by my mother; I found myself with hundreds of other villagers running into the woods. Machine-gun rounds were streaming over our heads. I could not understand what was going on. After a night of aimless running with one of my relatives... I came to a strange village where there were other children. In my innocence I asked, "Where am I?" and heard for the first time the word "Lebanon." After living the life of a refugee for more than a year, I was told one night that I would be returning home next day. We set out on the return journey. There were three of us: myself, my uncle, and the guide. After an exhausting journey I found myself in a village, but to my great disappointment, we had come to the village of Dair al-Asad, not to my village.
>
> When I came back from Lebanon, I was in the second class. The headmaster was an excellent man. When an Education Inspector visited the school, the headmaster would call me to his office and hide me in a narrow room, for the authorities would regard me as an interloper.
>
> Whenever the police came to the village, I would be hidden in a cupboard or in some corner or another because I was forbidden to live there, in my homeland. They protected me from informers by saying that I was in Lebanon. They taught me to say that I lived with one of the Bedouin tribes in the North. That is what I did to obtain the Israeli identity card.

Mahmoud Darwish completed his education in difficult circumstances, obtaining a General Secondary Certificate. He lived in the village of al-Djaydeh to which his family had moved, settling there in 1960. Mahmoud moved to Haifa where he began a new stage in his life. Faced with racialism and arrogance, and flagrant infringement of basic human rights, he became politically active, joining the Israeli Communist party. He made a living by writing for the Arabic newspaper published there, and subsequently worked on the newspaper *Al-Ittihad* and the magazine *Al-Jadid* (both organs of the Israeli Communist Party).

He frequently suffered arrest and imprisonment, first in 1961, in Haifa, and then in 1965, when he was imprisoned in a jail in Ramla, because he has traveled from Haifa to Jerusalem (to take part in an evening of poetry, organized by Arab students of Hebrew University in Jerusalem) without a permit from the Israeli authorities. He was jailed a third time in 1967, charged with engaging in "activities hostile to Israel." On the night of the Israeli aggression against neighboring Arab countries in June 1967, he was imprisoned in al-Damun jail. The fifth occasion was in 1969 when he was detained once again in Ramla.

At the beginning of 1970, he went to Moscow to study, thanks to the Israeli Communist Party. He stayed for over a year, and then went to Cairo in February 1971 having decided not to go back to Israel. In a public statement, he said, "The important step that I have taken stems from considerations of service to the cause: there are places where, it seems to me, there is more freedom and more liberty and which may allow me greater scope to express myself and to work than I could find in my own country. I am advancing from a place of restriction and imprisonment to a place of work. 'The hair of Mu'awiyah' connecting me to Israeli law has been broken; my ability to tolerate, to be patient, is now exhausted, especially since I no longer belong to a people that asks for mercy, that begs for alms, but to a people that fights."

In exile, he became editor-in-chief of the magazine *Shu'un Filastiniyyah* (Palestinian Affairs), published by the Center for Palestinian Research and Studies based in Beirut. After a while he left the magazine, and in 1987 he was elected to be a member of the executive committee of the PLO, and was made chairman of the Supreme Council for Culture, Education and Heritage. He resigned on

April 21, 1993, following the signing of the Oslo Accord between the PLO and Israel, and moved between a number of Arab and non-Arab capitals, finally settling in Beirut, which he left only after the Israeli military incursion in 1992. Subsequently, he lived in Tunis and Cyprus. He took the post of editor-in-chief of the magazine *Al-Karmel* and was long resident in Paris, which gave him the opportunity to explore the various cultures from around the world that co-exist there. In 1984, he was elected president of the Union of the Palestinian writers and journalists, and re-elected in 1987. He lived afterward partly in the Jordanian capital, Amman, and partly in Ramallah, in the West Bank.

Darwish's poetry has been translated into English, French, Russian, Swedish, German, Spanish, Dutch, Bulgarian, Hungarian, Polish, Italian, Persian, and Hebrew. He has been honored with the Lotus Prize by the Union of Afro-Asian Writers, the Ibn Sina Prize, the Lenin Peace Prize, the Mediterranean, the Shield of the Palestinian Revolution, the Spanish Library, France's Knight of Arts and Belles Lettres medal, the Officer Medal, a special prize from the International Cavafy Committee, the Lannan Prize for Cultural Freedom, the Dutch Prince Klaus, the Sultan Bin Ali Al 'Uwais Cultural Foundation prize, and the Arab Poetry Prize of the Supreme Council of Culture (Cairo) established by Naguib Mahfouz.

Mahmoud Darwish represents a unique poetic case in the field of Arabic poetry, beginning with the rise of modernism in the second half of the last century, up to the present day. Through his abundant creativity, he has been able to realize two things: he wrote genuinely popular poetry, at a time when Arabic poetry and its readership were both in decline; he preserved the spirit and values of poetry, while renewing and refining them, as no other writer was able to do. It has, perhaps, been his controversial popularization and originality that have made him "the Poet," one not to be confused with any other.

At the very beginning of his poetic career, Darwish was torn between two distinct phenomena: Palestinian resistance verse in opposition to the Israeli occupation and Arabic modernist verse, which was still exploring change and development in its full range. While Darwish and his poets were in quest for modernity in Arabic poetry, he quickly became, by the mid-1960s, the Palestinian Resistance Poet par excellence, striving to create a "national poem," while at the same time preserving the deep, human essence of poetry, which transcends context and is in tune with, as Wordsworth called it, "the still, sad music of humanity." It was possibly this striving, which gave his poetry a special dynamic, that led him to experiment with a new type of love poem that goes beyond both the sort of love poem that Nizar Qabbani made popular and the old Arabic love poem. By identifying the lost land of Palestine with his beloved, Darwish freed the traditional love poem from its narrower associations with lover and beloved, and imbued it with universal human values, deriving from love of the land, the meaning of love as it should be, and from the anguish of exile, human exile in its existential significance. Thus Darwish will oscillate in a poem which at first appears to be merely political agitation, between the national and the human, being aware as he was, from very early on, that the meaning of poetry lies in the contemplation of what is eternal and universal: love, death, and the boundless mystery of existence.

In his first phase, Darwish appears to be a romantic or a visionary poet, one who sees the beginnings and ends of things, combining in himself an assumed human position and one that is full of darkness. Even in this phase, which favored obscurity, he created a romantic style of poetry all his own, one that delights in all things and opens language up to new subjects, rather as if this strange romantic poet was clinging to his higher self and being exalted by it. The tension between the poetry that relates to all existence and the poetry that sees itself as one of its aspects, an astonishing linguistic explosion—this tension is a feature of Darwish's poetry. All this, in the absence of any claim that poetry is an activity of language and that poetic language breaks through and transcends reality.

If such modernist poets as Qabbani and al-Sayyab draw the inspiration for their poetry from modern subjects, or from language itself, avoiding the everyday and the immediately tangible, Mahmoud Darwish creates his language from a broad contemplation of life, which gives his poetry a spacious vividness, and from a constant dialogue with "the prestigious reader" who has expectations of the poet and whom the poet invites to come with him into the enlightening of poetry, as it should be. In this way, the reader occupies a place of privilege in the continuation of a poem by Darwish, not in the simple programmatic sense, but in that of the "poetic question" that anticipates an aesthetic answer. The answer lies in linguistic aesthetics that combine surface simplicity and amazing intensity, with the questions of both reader and poet. This produces a multilayered text that belongs at the same time to the reader and to great poetry. Thus, Darwish's text appears as a fabric made up of metaphor and dynamic symbolism, combined with verse that approximates prose, or prose that approximates verse, not in the technical sense, though, but in the sense of an unconditional search for the meaning and identity of poetry.

Darwish began by writing poems about Palestine, and, after long explorations of obscurity, has arrived at a human poetic enterprise, in which he contemplates the seven ancient *Mu'allaqat*, and writes *al-Jidariya*, looking to the poetic heritage of mankind as a whole. Thus, his collection *Ward Aqal* (Fewer Roses) tended toward "private verse" and this tendency became more pronounced in this collection, *Kazahr al-lawz aw ab'ad* (*Almond Blossoms and Beyond*). At the same time, these collections, like the collection *Anthuru ila ma ureed* ("I See What I Want") are Palestinian poems, which extend into his collection *Halat Hisar* ("A State of Siege"), where the man is visible in the Palestinian, where the Palestinian, as a human subject, shares the experience of love and grief, of future expectations, and of the inevitable fear of the impending moment of annihilation, with the rest of mankind.

Critics describe Darwish as "multifarious," a poet who is in conversation with both classical and modern Arabic poetry, who has meditated on the subjects of life in many poetic forms, and with great spontaneity. The diversity to be found in his poems is not to be separated from a multicultural poetic enterprise that embraces the Arab, Islamic, European, Jewish, and Greek culture in a fertile multiplicity that expresses love and tolerance, and which reveals in the poem the substance of a man, with all his inherent creative possibility.

—*Mohammad Shaheen*

"Fine speech manifests its image
in poetics as though it were prose,
and in prose as though it were poetic."

—Abu Hayyan al-Tawhidi
Al-Emta' wal –Mu'anasah

(Enjoyment and Entertainment)
"The Twenty-Fifth Night"

. I .

YOU

Think of Others

As you prepare your breakfast, think of others
(do not forget the pigeon's food).
As you wage your wars, think of others
(do not forget those who seek peace).
As you pay your water bill, think of others
(those who are nursed by clouds).
As you return home, to your home, think of others
(do not forget the people of the camps).
As you sleep and count the stars, think of others
(those who have nowhere to sleep).
As you express yourself in metaphor, think of others
(those who have lost the right to speak).
As you think of others far away, think of yourself
(say: *If only I were a candle in the dark*).

Now, in Exile

Now, in exile…yes, at home.
At sixty, in a fleeting life,
they are lighting candles for you.

So rejoice as calmly as you are able,
because Death has strayed and missed you
in the crowds… he put off his visit.

An inquisitive moon on the ruins laughs like a fool
so do not believe that which comes close to meet you.
He, in his old job, like the new March,
returned to the trees names of longing
and ignored you.

So celebrate with your friends and break the glass.
At sixty you will find no tomorrow waiting
to carry on the shoulder of anthem,
and for him to carry you.

Say to life, as befits a mature poet:
Move leisurely, as a woman confident in her own charm
and cunning. For each one some secret call:
Come here, how lovely you are!

Move leisurely, Life, so that I can see you
with all the loss about me. How much I have forgotten you
in your crossways, seeking me and you. Whenever
I grasped one of your secrets, you would sternly say:
How ignorant you are!

Say to those who are distant: You have reduced me.
I am here to complete you!

When You Gaze Long

When you gaze long at a rose
that has wounded a wall, you say to yourself:
I hope for a cure from the sand.
    Your heart turns green…

When you take a woman to the circus,
a woman whose day is lovely as an icon…
and you dismount like a guest to the horse's prance.
    your heart turns red…

When you count the stars, and make a mistake after
thirteen, and you doze like a child
in the blue of the night,
    your heart turns white…

When you journey, and do not find the dream
that walks before you like a shadow,
    your heart turns yellow…

If You Walk on a Street

If you walk on a street that does not lead to an abyss,
say to the garbage collector, *Thank you!*

If you come back home alive, as rhyme returns,
unharmed, say to yourself, *Thank you!*

If you have expected something, and your guess has deceived you,
go tomorrow to see where you were, and say to the butterfly, *Thank you!*

If you have cried out with all your might, and the echo replied,
Who is there? say to identity, *Thank you!*

If you have looked at a rose without it causing you pain,
and you have rejoiced in it, say to your heart , *Thank you!*

If you wake in the morning and find no one around you
to rub your eyelids, say to sight, *Thank you!*

If you remember a letter of your name and the name of your country,
    be a good child!
So that the Lord will say to you, *Thank you!*

A Café, and You with the Newspaper

A café, and you with the newspaper, sitting.
No, you are not alone. Your cup half full,
and the sun filling the other half...
Through the window, you see hurrying passersby,
but you are unseen. (That's one of the
attributes of invisibility: you see but are not seen.)
How free you are, forgotten man in the café!
No one to see how the violin affects you.
No one to stare at your presence or your absence,
or to gaze into your fog if you look
at a girl and are broken before her.
How free you are, minding your business
in this crowd, with none to watch or read you!
Do what you will with yourself.
Take off your shirt or your shoes.
If you want, you are forgotten and free in your imagination.
There is no pressing work for your name or your face here.
You are as you are—no friend, no enemy here to study your memoirs.
Seek forgiveness for the one who left you in this café
because you did not notice her new hairstyle,
and the butterflies dancing on her temples.
Seek forgiveness for the man who sought
to murder you one day, for no reason,
or because you did not die the day
you bumped into a star and wrote
those early songs with its ink.
A café, and you with the newspaper, sitting
in the corner, forgotten. No one to insult
your peaceful state of mind and no one to think of murdering you.
How forgotten you are,
how free in your imagination!

. II .

HE

He and None Other

He, and none other, who dismounted from a star
that had done him no harm.
He said: My legend will not survive long,
nor my image in the people's imagination.
So let the truth test me.
I said to him: If you appear, you will be broken—
do not let that happen.
His prophetic pain said to me: Where am I going?
I said: To an invisible star, or to the cave.
He said: I am obsessed by a reality I cannot decipher.
I said: Then record your memories of the distant star,
of a tomorrow slow in coming. Ask
your imagination whether it knew
that this journey of yours would be so long.
He said: But my friend, I am not good at writing!
Were you lying to us, then? I asked.
And he replied: The dream must guide the dreamers
like inspiration—and with a sigh—
Take my hand, impossible thing!
And he disappeared, as legends do.
He did not win to die, nor lose to live.
Take our hands, impossible thing!

He Waited for No One

He waited for no one. He felt no lack in existence.
Before him a river, ashen as his overcoat,
and sunlight filling his heart with awakening brightness
and the tall trees

He felt no defect in the place.
The wooden seat, his coffee,
the glass of water, the strangers;
everything in the café the same.

Nothing had changed. Even the newspapers
yesterday's news, and an old world floating as usual on the dead.
He felt no need for hope to amuse him
like the unknown growing green in the desert
or some wolf longing for a guitar.

He expected nothing, not even a surprise,
he could not cope with repetition.
I knew the end of the journey from the first step,
he says to himself.
I have not withdrawn from the world,
nor have I gotten closer to the world.

He waited for no one, and he felt no defect
in his senses. Autumn was still his royal host,
luring him with music that returned him
to a golden age of awakening,
to poetry rhyming with stars and space.

He waited for no one in front of the river

In the no-waiting, I become an in-law to the sparrow.
In the no-waiting, I become a river—he said—
I am not hard on myself.
I am not hard on anyone.

And I escape the serious question:
What do you want
What do you want?

Orange-Like

Orange-like, the sun enters the sea
the orange is a water lamp on cold trees.

Orange-like, the sun gives birth to the divine child of sunset
and the orange, one of her maidens, contemplates her unknown.

Orange-like, the sun pours its liquid into the mouth of the sea
and the orange is fearful of a hungry mouth.

Orange-like, the sun enters eternity's cycles,
and the orange wins the praise of her killer:
    that fruit which is like a piece of sun
    is peeled by hand and mouth, is hoarse of taste.
    The chatterbox of perfume, drunk with her liquid…
    Her color is like nothing else,
    her color, like the sun in sleep.
    Her color is her taste: sour, sweet,
    rich in the health of light and vitamin C…

There is no reason why poetry
should not falter in telling its story and beware of
an amazing flaw in the image.

A Wedding over There

There is a wedding two doors down from us
so don't shut the door; don't put a screen between us
and the surge of strange joy.
If a rose withers, the spring does not feel
a duty to lament. If the sick nightingale
is silent, the canary lends its share of song.
And if a star falls, the sky is not hurt.
There is a wedding over there,
so do not shut the door in the face of this air,
perfumed with ginger and ripe bridal peach.
She weeps and laughs like water. (Water is not wounded.
There is no trace of the blood that flowed in the night.)
It is said: Love is as strong as Death.
I say: But lust for life, even with no satisfying proofs,
is stronger than Life and Death.
So let us end our private funeral rite
and share with our neighbors in song.
Life is axiomatic… and true as dust.

Wide Space

Wide space. Copper. Small brown birds.
A willow tree. Idleness. Horizon unnoticed as in great sagas.
Wrinkled face of earth. Summer yawning like a dog
in the dry shade of an olive tree. Sweat on the rock,
vertical sun. No life, no death hereabouts.
Dryness, like the smell of light in the wheat.
No water in the well or the heart.
No love in lovemaking—like patriotic duty,
that's love.
A native's desert, invisible behind this dryness.
Dryness like the freedom of prisoners, cleaning
their badges with bird droppings.
Dryness like the divine right
bestowed on husbands over their wives,
wantonly deserted in beds.
No green grass, no yellow grass.
No color in the sickness of color.
Everywhere the color of ashes.

No waiting, then, for the barbarians
on their way to us, on the eve
of the celebration honoring our country!

. III .

I

These Are the Words

These are the words that flutter about in the mind.
In the mind is heavenly earth, word-borne.
The dead do not dream much, and if they do,
no one believes their dreams…
These words swarm in my body as a bee
as a bee… Had I written blue on blue, the songs
would have turned green, and my life returned to me.
In words, I found the path to the names shorter.
Poets do not rejoice much, and if they do,
no one would say they are right.
I said: I am still alive, because I see the words fluttering about in the mind.
In the mind, the song oscillates between presence
and absence, opens the door only to shut it.
A song about the life of fog, though, obeys
only the words I have forgotten.

To Describe an Almond Blossom

To describe an almond blossom no encyclopedia of flowers
is any help to me, no dictionary.
Words carry me off to snares of rhetoric
that wound the sense, and praise the wound they've made.
Like a man telling a woman her own feeling.
How can the almond blossom shine in my own language,
when I am but an echo?
It is translucent, like liquid laughter that has sprouted
on boughs out of the shy dew...
light as a white musical phrase. . .
weak as the glance of a thought that peeks out from our fingers
as in vain we write it...
dense as a line of verse not arranged alphabetically.
To describe an almond blossom, I need to make visits to the unconscious,
which guides me to affectionate names hanging on trees.
What is its name?
What is the name of this thing in the poetics of nothing?
I must break out of gravity and words,
in order to feel their lightness when they turn
into whispering ghosts, and I make them as they make me,
a white translucence.
Neither *homeland* nor *exile* are words,
but passions of whiteness in a
description of the almond blossom.
Neither snow nor cotton.
One wonders how it rises above things and names.
If a writer were to compose a successful piece
describing an almond blossom, the fog would rise
from the hills, and people, all the people, would say:
    This is it.
    These are the words of our national anthem.

I Sit at Home

I sit at home, not sad, not happy,
not myself, or anyone else.

Scattered newspapers.
The roses in the vase do not remind me
of who plucked them for me.
Today is a holiday from memory,
a holiday from everything…
    Today is Sunday.

The day when we put our kitchen and bedroom in order.
Everything in its place. We listen to the news
calmly. No war is being raged.

The happy emperor plays with his dogs,
drinks champagne from between ivory breasts,
and swims in foam.

The sole emperor today takes his siesta,
like me, and like you. He does not think of Resurrection—
he holds it in his right hand, and it is truth and eternity.

Weak, lightweight, my coffee boils.
Cardamom fills the air and the body.

It is as if I were alone. I am he
or I am the other. He saw me and was reassured
about my day and departed.

Sunday
is the first day in the Torah, but
time changes customs for the Lord
of War now rests on Sundays.

I sit in the house, not happy, not sad, betwixt and between.
I would not care if I were to learn
that I am not really myself... or anyone else!

I Love Autumn and the Shade of Meanings

I love autumn and the shade of meanings.
Delighted in autumn by a light obscurity,
transparency of handkerchiefs, like poetry just after
birth, dazzled in night-blaze or darkness.
It crawls, and finds no names for anything.

Shy rain, which moistens only distant things,
delights me.
(In such autumns, marriage procession
and funeral intersect: the living
celebrate with the dead, and the dead
celebrate with the living.)

I delight to see a monarch stoop,
to recover the pearl of the crown from a fish in the lake.

In autumn I delight to see the commonness of colors,
no throne holds the humble gold in the leaves of humble trees
who are equal in the thirst for love.

I delight in the truce between armies,
awaiting the contest between two poets,
who love the season of autumn, yet differ
over the direction of its metaphors.

In autumn I delight in the complicity between
vision and expression.

As for Spring

As for spring, whatever drunken poets write when
they succeed to catch fleeting time with a hook
of words... they sober up, unharmed.

A little cold in the coal of the pomegranate
eases the sting of fire in the metaphor. (If I were nearer
to me than you, I would kiss myself.)

A little color in the almond blossom
protects the heavens from the heathen's
last arguments. (However we differ, we
realize happiness is possible, as is an earthquake.)

A little dancing among the plants at a licentious
wedding feast stimulates our blood.
(The seed does not know death,
no matter how far we go.)

Eternity is shy of no one
when she grants her body to all
here... in the fleeting spring.

I Used to Love Winter

In the past, I was inclined to honor winter,
and I listen to my body.
Rain, rain, like a love letter pours licentiously
from the imprudent heavens.
Winter. A cry. An echo
hungry for the embrace of women.
In the distance, the steamy breath
of a horse carrying clouds... white, white.
I used to love winter, to walk joyfully to my
rendezvous in space drenched in water.
My love used to dry my short hair with
Long hair luxuriant with wheat and chestnuts.
She was not content with singing,
I and winter love you,
    so stay with us!
She would warm my heart
on two hot gazelle fawns.
I used to love winter,
and I would listen to it,
drop by drop.
Rain, rain like an appeal to a lover,
Pour down my body!
Winter was no lament pointing
to the end of life. It was the beginning. It was hope.
So what shall I do, as life falls like hair?
What will I do this winter?

As If I Were Joyful

As if I were joyful, I returned.
I rang the doorbell more than once, waited…
Perhaps I was late. No one opened.
Not a sound in the corridor.
I remembered I had my keys.
I apologized to myself—
    I'm sorry, I forgot you. Go on in.
We entered… I was guest and host
in my own home. I looked at everything in the empty space,
I searched and found no trace of myself,
perhaps… perhaps I wasn't there.
I found no image of myself in the mirrors.
So, I thought, where am I?
I cried to wake myself from delirium,
but could not. I was broken,
a voice rolling on the floor.
I asked, Why then did I come back?
And I apologized to myself—I forgot about you,
go away! But I could not.
I walked to my bedroom, and the dream
came at me in a rush and embraced me, asking,
    Have you changed?
I said, I have changed. To die at home
is better than to be crushed by a car
in the street, in an empty square.

Happy (I Know Not Why)

With joy at something secret I used to embrace
the morning with the strength of singing and walk with confidence
in my steps, walk with confidence in my visions.
Some inspiration calls me: Come on!
Like a magic gesture, like a dream come to train me in its secrets
so that I may be the master of my star in the night...
relying on my language.
I am my own dream, I am; I am my mother's mother in looks;
and my father's father; and
my son, I am.

With joy at something secret,
carrying me on stringed
singing instruments to polish me like the diamonds of
an Eastern princess.
    If the world does not break into song now,
    on this morning,
    it will never sing.

Love, give us your abundance, that we may plunge
into the noble wars of those who feel strongly.
The climate is favorable
and the sun sharpens our weapons in the morning.
Love! We have no aim but defeat in your wars...
Triumph, you are Triumph.
Hear your praise from your victims, Triumph!
May your hands be safe.
Return safely to us when we are lost!

With joy at something secret, I was walking,
dreaming a blue poem of two lines.
Two lines... about a light joy at once visible and secret:
    He who does not love now,
    on this morning,
    will never love!

I Do Not Know the Stranger

I do not know the stranger or his exploits.
I saw the procession and followed the coffin
like the others, with head respectfully bowed.
I found no reason to ask, Who is this stranger?
Where did he live? How did he die?
(There are many causes of death,
among them the ache of life.)
I asked myself, Does he see us, or does he see
annihilation? Does he regret the end?
I knew that he would not open the coffin,
covered with violets, to say goodbye to us,
and thank us, and whisper the truth.
(What is the truth?) Perhaps he is in these hours,
like us, rolling up his shadow.
But he was the one person who did not lament this morning.
He did not see death hovering over us like a hawk.
(The living are the cousins of the dead, and the dead
sleep peacefully, peacefully, peacefully.) I found no
cause to ask, Who is the stranger and what is his name?
(No lightning flash in his name.)
Twenty walk behind him, apart from me.
(I am another.)
I wondered in my heart at the door of the church:
Was he a writer, a worker, a refugee,
a thief, or a murderer? What is the difference?
The dead are all alike in the face of death.
They do not talk and perhaps do not dream.
Perhaps the stranger's funeral is my funeral, but some divine
decree has postponed my death
for many reasons, among them a serious mistake in the poem!

. IV .

SHE

Beautiful Women Are Beautiful Women

Beautiful women are beautiful women
(violin-shaped in the waist).
Beautiful women are weak women
(small throne without memory).
Beautiful women are powerful women
(despair enlightens and does not burn).
Beautiful women are princesses
(anxious muses).
Beautiful women are near
(neighbors of the rainbow).
Beautiful women are beyond our reach
(a song of joy).
Beautiful women are poor women
(roses on the battlefield).
Beautiful women are lonely women
(maids-of-honor before the queen).
Beautiful women are tall women
(aunts of the palms of the sky).
Beautiful women are short women
(a glass of water downed at once).
Beautiful women are old women
(peeled mangos and mature wine).
Beautiful women are little women
(tomorrow's promise and lily buds).
Beautiful women—all beautiful women—*you*,
if they met to choose
for me the noblest of women martyrs.

Like a Small Café, That's Love

Like a small café on the street of strangers—
that's love... its doors open to all.
Like a café that expands and
contracts with the weather:
if it pours with rain its customers increase,
if the weather's fine, they are few and weary...
I am here, stranger, sitting in the corner.
(What color are your eyes? What is your name?
How shall I call to you as you pass by,
as I sit waiting for you?)
A small café, that's love.
I order two glasses of wine
and drink to my health and yours.
I am carrying two caps
and an umbrella. It is raining now.
It is raining more than ever,
and you do not come in.
I say to myself at last: Perhaps she who I was waiting for
was waiting for me, or was waiting for some other man,
or was waiting for us, and did not find him/me.
She would say: Here I am waiting for you.
(What color are your eyes? What is your name?
What kind of wine do you prefer? How shall I call to you when
you pass by?)
          A small café, that's love...

A Hand That Scatters Wakefulness

A hand that scatters the wakefulness white, and stays late at night,
that forbids and commands, that is far-off and near,
stern and sympathetic.
A hand that breaks the azure with a gesture,
and makes horses dance on *An-nahawnad.**
A hand that is exalted. That chatters when speech dries up.
A hand that pours lightning in a cup of tea,
milks the udder of a cloud,
flatters the flute: *You are my echo.*
A hand that predicts what will soon happen.
A hand that glimmers in five stars.
That forbids night its due of drowsiness.
A hand that squeezes words to yield water.
A hand that narrates the migration of birds from it, to it.
A hand that raises the spirit in words. A hand
that orders the army to sleep in barracks. A hand
that shifts the waves in my body. Her hand is a
whisper that touches the highest note:
Take me... here and now... take me!

An-nahawnad: A musical note.

I Wish I Were Younger

He: I wish I were younger—
She: I shall grow older by night, like the scent
of jasmine in summer. And you will grow
young when you sleep: all sleepers are young.
But I shall keep vigilance till morning, till
there are patches beneath my eyes. Two threads
of perfect tiredness suffice for me to begin to age.
I shall squeeze a lemon over my belly to disguise
the scent of milk and cotton.
I will rub my breasts with salt and ginger till they swell more.
He: There is no room in the heart for the garden,
my child... And no time in my body for the morrow.
So grow up quietly and slowly.
She: Love does not listen to advice. Take me,
so that I may grow up! Take me
so that you may grow young.
He: When you grow up, tomorrow you will say,
I wish I were younger—
She: My desire is like a fruit that will not
last. There is no time in my body to wait till tomorrow!

I Do Not Sleep to Dream

I do not sleep to dream,
she told him. I sleep to forget you.
How good it is to sleep alone,
soundless in silk. Withdraw, so that I may see you
alone there. Think of me while I forget you.
I feel no pain from your absence;
neither the night nor your lips scratch my breast.
I sleep in my body utterly, sharing with no one.
Your hands do not tear my dress, nor do your feet.
Your feet knock against my heart like a rifle
as you shut the door.
I am in need of nothing in your absence.
My breasts are my own, my navel, my freckles, my mole,
my hands and my legs are my own.
Everything of mine is mine.
Keep the sensual pictures you took,
take them to entertain your exile,
and raise your fantasies like
a last toast. Say, if you wish, that passion is mortal.

But I shall listen to my body,
    quietly, like a doctor. Nothing, nothing in your absence
    causes me pain, except for the isolation of being!

She Forgot a Cloud in the Bed

She forgot a cloud in the bed.
She left quickly and said, *I will forget you.*
But she forgot a cloud in the bed.
I covered it with the silk sheet and said to her,
Do not fly, do not follow her;
      she will return to you.
(There were birds, blue, yellow, red, drinking from a cloud
moving slowly as it showed itself over her shoulders.)
She will realize when she returns home, without
an escort of birds, that the atmosphere has changed
over the coast of her shoulders,
and that the clouds have evaporated.
Then she will remember what she forgot:
a cloud in my bed
and she will return to reclaim
her royal customs in a cloud.
            So I scolded her and smiled,
and when I got into bed to lie down
in the metaphor, the water made me wet.

She/He

She: Have you ever known love?
He: When winter comes,
I will be touched
by a passion for
something absent.
I will give it a name,
any name,
and will forget...
She: What will you forget? Tell me!
He: The fevered shiver, my raving
beneath the sheets as I sigh, *Cover me,*
cover me!
She: What you are talking about
is not love.
He: What I am talking about
is not love.
She: Have you ever felt the desire
to pass through death
in a woman's arms?
He: The more complete the absence
the more I am present. Distance is shattered,
and death embraces life, and life
embraces death... like lovers.
She: Then what?
He: Then what?
She: You were united with her
and you did not know her hands
from yours.
You both evaporated
like a blue cloud
without showing you were
two bodies, two reflections, or... ?
He: Who is the female?—A metaphor of earth in us?
Who is the male?—The sky?

She: That is how love songs begin.
So you once knew love!
He: The more perfect the presence
and the more the unknown
is tamed, the more I am absent.
She: It is winter.
Perhaps I have become the past
you prefer in winter.
He: Perhaps… *au revoir*.
She: Perhaps… *au revoir*!

She Does Not Love You

She does not love you.
Your metaphors thrill her.
You are her poet.
But that's all there is to it.

She is thrilled by the river,
plunging in rhythm.
So become a river to thrill her!
She is thrilled by the union
of lightning and sound
in your rhyme…
Her breasts drip
on a letter.
So become the first letter of the alphabet
to excite her!
She is excited by the elevation of things,
from anything to light,
from a light to ringing,
from ringing to feeling.
So become one of her emotions to excite her.

She is excited by the struggle
of her night with her breasts.
(Love, you have tormented me.
O river pouring its ferocious sensuality
outside my room.
O Love! If you do not bless me with lust,
I will kill you.)

Be an angel,
not to impress her with your metaphor,
but so that she may kill you
to avenge her femininity
and escape the snare of metaphor.

Perhaps she has come to love you
since you raised her to the sky,
and you became another person,
occupying the highest throne in her sky.
And there, matters became confused
among the stars, between Pisces and Virgo.

She Has Not Come

She has not come,
I said, and will not come.
So I will arrange my evening
as befits my disappointment and
her absence.
I put out the flame of her candles,
and turned on the electric light.
I drank her glass of wine
and smashed it.
I changed the sound of frenetic violins
to Persian songs.
I said, *She will not come*.
I will loosen my smart tie (that's much better)
and put on blue pajamas.
I will walk barefoot if I want.
I will squat down at my ease on her sofa
and forget her, and forget everything that is not here.
I returned all the things that I got out for our party
to their drawers.
I opened all my windows and curtains.
No secrets in my body as I face the night,
except what I had expected and lost.
I laughed at the way
I freshened the air for her, like a fool.
(I used a rosewater and lemon spray.)
She will not come.
I will move her orchid plant
from right to left
to punish her for her forgetfulness.
I covered up the looking glass on the wall
with a coat, so as not to see
the radiance of her picture and regret it.
I said: I better forget what I quoted for her
from the old ghazal, because

she does not deserve a poem,
not even one that has been pirated.
I have forgotten her,
eaten a quick meal while standing,
and I have read a chapter
of a schoolbook about remote stars.
And I wrote,
so as to forget her offense,
a poem. This poem!

When You Are With Me

When you are with me, I do not say:
here and now we are together.
Rather, I say: You and I and eternity,
we swim in nowhere.

Air and water.
We solve the riddles.
We name. We are named
and we do not speak,
except to learn how like us we are
and to forget time.

I do not remember in which land you were born.
I do not remember from which land I was resurrected.
Air and water,
and we are flying on a star.

When you are with me silence sweats.
The clear sky is bathed in cloud.
The water weeps,
and the air weeps,
when two bodies are united.

There is no love in love,
but the soul's lust for flight.

Now, After You

Now, after you, with an appropriate rhyme
and exile, the trees improve their posture and laugh.
It is summer in autumn: like a holiday
at the wrong time, a hole in time,
like the breaking-off of a song.

Summer in autumn.
    The days turn toward a green garden
    whose fruit is not ripe.
    Toward a story that is not finished.
    In us, two seagulls hover
    from the distant to the more-distant.

The sun laughs in the streets.
    Women get out of bed laughing, laughing,
    bathing in their inner sun, naked, naked.
It is autumn's summer, which comes
from new extra time.

It is summer in autumn that binds me and binds you—
Wait! Perhaps a different and better ending awaits
    you in front of the metro station.
    Perhaps another beginning enters the café
    and does not leave after you.
    Perhaps some love letter is delayed in the post.

But now, after you,
with a suitable rhyming and exile, the trees improve
their posture and laugh.
I long for you. I long for you
    when you are bathing, far off in your sun.

It is summer in autumn,
a holiday at the wrong time.

We will know that it is a season that defends
its importance and happy mythical love…

The sun laughs and laughs at our folly.
    I will not return,
    and you will not return!

. V .

EXILE 1

Tuesday, a Bright Day

Tuesday, a bright day. I walk
along a side street, roofed over by
chestnut trees. I walk lightly, lightly,
as if I had evaporated from my body, as if
I had an appointment with a poem.
I look at my watch, absent-minded.
I leaf through distant clouds, which register lofty ideas in the sky.
My heart's affairs
I turn over to a walnut tree: without
electricity like a small
hut on the seashore.
Faster, slower, faster I walk.
I gaze at the signs on either side...
I do not recall the words. I hum a tune,
slowly, as the unemployed do: The river
runs like a foal to its fate, the sea.
The birds snatch seeds from the shoulders of the river.
And I mutter, mutter in secret: Live tomorrow now!
However long you might live you will not reach tomorrow.
There is no land for tomorrow. Dream slowly,
and whatever you dream, understand
that the moth does not burn to give you light.

I walk lightly, lightly, looking about me.
Perhaps I will see a likeness between my self
and the willow tree in this place.
But I can make out nothing here that refers to me.

> *(If the canary does not sing to you, my friend,*
> *know that you are your own jailer,*
> *if the canary does not sing.)*

No land is as narrow as a flowerpot,
like your land. No land is wide

as the book, as your own land. And your visions
are your exile in a world where a shadow has
no identity, no gravity.

You walk as if you were someone else.

If I could speak to someone on the road, I would say,
My peculiarity is what does not point to myself,
and what is not named, from death,
a dream, nothing more.
If I could speak to a woman on the road, I would say,
My peculiarity does not arouse attention:
the calcifying of some arteries in the feet, nothing more.
And so walk with me, walk slowly, like a cloud,
neither dawdling nor hurrying.

If I could speak to the specter of death
behind the azalea hedge, I would say,
We were born together as twins—you, who would kill me,
are my brother. You, who are the designer of my course on this earth
(my mother and yours), throw down your weapon.

If I could speak to love after lunch, I would say,
When we were lads, we had dexterous hands,
with unfeathered words, fainting on two knees.
You had few qualities, quite active and clearer.
Your face is the face of an angel come from sleep;
and your body is a ram with the power of a fever.
You were called as you were, Love, and we fainted
and the night fainted.

I walk lightly, and grow older
by ten minutes, twenty, sixty.
I walk and the life in me
slips gently away, like a light cough.
I think,

What if I were to slow down, what if I were to stop?
Would I stop time? Would I upset death?
I laugh at my idea.

Then I ask myself,
Where are you going, confident as an ostrich?
I walk as if life someday makes good its deficiencies.
I don't look back, for I can return to nothing,
and can be no other.

If I could speak to the Lord, I would say:
My Lord, my God! Why hast Thou forsaken me?
I am only the shadow of your shadow on earth.
How couldst Thou forsake me, and cause me to fall
into the snares of a question:
Why didst Thou create mosquitoes,
my God, my God?

I walk, going nowhere in particular,
without tomorrow's promises.
I remember that I had forgotten,
and I forget as I remember.

I forget a crow on an olive branch;
I remember an olive stain on a garment.

I forget the call of the gazelle to its mate;
I remember a line of ants on the sand.

I forget my longing for a star that's fallen from my hand;
I remember the fur of foxes.

I forget the old road to our house;
I remember an emotion like a tangerine.

I forget what it was I said;

I remember what I have not said yet.

I forget my grandfather's stories, and a sword on a wall;
I remember my fear of sleep.

I forget the girl's lips filled with grapes;
I remember the smell of lettuce between fingers.

I forget the houses that have marked out my life;
I remember the identity-card number.

I forget big events and a devastating earthquake;
I remember my father's tobacco in the cupboard.

I forget the paths of departing to nothingness;
I remember the starlight in the Bedouin encampments.

I forget the whine of bullets in the deserted village;
I remember the song of crickets in the woods.

I forget as I remember, and I remember what I have forgotten.

(But I
remember
this day;
Tuesday, a
bright day.)

And I walk down a street that leads to no destination.
Perhaps my footsteps have guided me
to an empty bench in the garden, or
perhaps they've guided me to an idea about the truth lost
between the aesthetic and the real.
I sit alone, as if I had a rendezvous
with one of the women of imagination.
I imagined that I waited for so long

that I was exasperated, and burst out,
    Why are you late?
She lies:
The crowd was thick on the bridge.
    So calm down.
I will calm down when she fondles my hair.
I will feel that the garden is our private chamber,
        and the shadows curtains.

(If the canary does not sing to you, my friend,
know that you have slept too long,
if the canary does not sing.)

She asks: What are you saying?
I say: The canary does not sing to me.
Do you remember me, stranger?
Am I like that old pastoral poet,
who the stars crowned King of the Night...
the one who abdicated his throne and was
sent off to be shepherd of the clouds?
She says: Is it possible that this day is like yesterday?
As if you were...

There on that wooden bench, opposite,
is a girl, heartbroken from waiting.
She drinks a glass of fruit juice
and polishes the crystal of my heart,
and takes from me today's emotion.

I ask her: How did you get here?
She says: I came by chance. I was walking
down a street that leads to no destination.
I say: I walked as if I had an appointment...
perhaps my footsteps led me to an empty bench
in the garden, or to an idea
about the truth lost between imagination and reality.

She says: Do you also remember me, stranger?
Am I like yesterday's woman, that young girl
with the braid, and the short songs
of love after a long sleep?
I say: As if you were—

(A young man now comes through the garden gate,
carrying twenty-five lilies for the girl who waited for him—
he takes from me this day's youth.)

A small thing is the heart, my heart.
A big thing is love, my love.

It travels on the wind, comes down,
peels a pomegranate, then falls
into the maze of two almond eyes,
rises out of two dimples,
and forgets the way back to home and name.

A small thing is the heart, my heart.
    A big thing is love.

Was it I who was he?
    Or was he who I never was?

She asks: Why do clouds scrape the tops of trees?
I say: Because legs cling to one another in the drizzling rain.

She asks: Why does a frightened cat stare at me?
I say: So that you stop the storm.

She says: Why does the stranger long for yesterday?
I say: So that poetry can be independent.

She asks: Why does the sky turn ashen in the evening?
I say: Because you have not watered the flowers.

She asks: Why do you mock?
I say: So that the song finds a little bread to feed on
from time to time.

She asks: Why do we love and walk on empty roads?
I say: To conquer a lot of death with a little death,
and to escape the abyss.

She asks: Why did I dream that I saw a swallow in my hand?
I say: Because you need someone.

She asks: Why do you remind me of a tomorrow that I will not see
you in?
I say: Because you are an attribute of eternity.

She says: You will pass alone into the tunnel of night alone after I
am gone.
I say: I will pass into the tunnel of night after you are gone, alone.

...And I walk heavily, heavily,
as if I had an appointment with one of the losses.
I walk with the poet in me,
preparing for his eternal rest
in a London night.
My friend on the way to Damascus!
We have not yet reached Syria.
Do not hurry, do not hurry.
Do not orphan the jasmine.
Do not subject me to the test of a dirge!
How should I bear the burden of a poem
about you and about me?

The poem of those who do not like to describe fog
is his poem.
The coat of clouds over the church
is his coat.

The secret of two hearts taking refuge in Barada
is his secret.
The palm tree of Sumer, mother of songs,
is his tree.
The keys of Cordoba, south of the clouds,
are his keys.
He does not round off his poems with his own name.
The young girl knows him,
if she feels the prick of the pin,
and the salt in her blood.
Like mine, his heart pursues him.
Like him, I do not round off my will
with my own name.
The wind knows my family's new address,
at the foot of an abyss in the far south.
Goodbye, my friend, goodbye.
Greet Damascus for me.

I am not young enough to be carried away by words.
I am not young enough to finish this poem.

I walk by night with the *daad*.*
That is my linguistic peculiarity—I walk
with the night accompanied by the *daad*,
a middle-aged man spurring on an old horse
to fly to the Eiffel Tower.
O my language, help me to learn
so that I may embrace the universe.
Inside me is a balcony,
which no one passes to greet me.
Outside of me is a world,
which does not return my greeting.
O my language, am I what you are?
Or are you, my language, what I am?
O my language, prepare me
for the nuptials of the alphabet

daad: Arabic letter "D"

and my body.
Let me be a lord, not an echo!
Cover me with your wool.
O my language, help me to differ so that I may
achieve harmony. Give birth to me
and I will give birth to you.

I am your son sometimes,
and sometimes, your father and mother.
If you are, I am, and if I am, you are.

O my language,
call this new age by foreign names
and invite the distant stranger to be your guest,
invite the simple prose of life
to ripen my verse.
For who, if I don't speak in poetry,
will understand me?
Who will speak to me
of hidden longing for a lost age
if I don't speak in poetry?
And who, if I don't speak in poetry,
will know the stranger's land?

The night is calm. The night is complete.
A flower was awoken to breathe by the garden fence.
I said: I will testify that I am alive, even from afar.
And that I dreamed that he who was dreaming was none
other than myself.
And my day, Tuesday, was spacious and long,
and my night like a short encore I added
to the play after the curtain was down.
But I shall harm no one if I add,
    It was a beautiful day,
    like a true love story on an express train.

(If the canary does not sing to you, my friend,
blame no one but yourself.
If the canary does not sing to you,
then you yourself sing to it.
Sing to it.)

. VI .

EXILE 2

With the Fog So Dense on the Bridge

With the fog so dense on the bridge, he said to me,
Is anything known to the contrary?
I said, At dawn, things will be clear.
He said, There is no time more obscure than dawn.
Let your imagination succumb
to the river.
In the blue dawn, in the prison yard
or near the pine wood, a young man is executed, hopeful of victory.
In the blue dawn, the smell of bread
draws a map of a life whose summer is more like spring.
In the blue dawn, dreamers wake gently
and merrily walk in the waters of their dream.

Where is dawn taking us?
Dawn is a bridge; where does it take us?

My friend said to me,
I do not want a place to be buried in.
I want a place to live in and curse, if I wish.

Place passes like a gesture between us—
    What is *place*? I asked.

Senses discovering a footprint of intuition, he said.
Then he sighed, Oh, for that narrow street
that carried me in the ample evening
to her house on the outskirts of solitude.
Do you still keep my heart in memory
and forget the smoke of the city?

Don't bet on reality, I told him.
You will find nothing alive like its own image awaiting you.
Time tames even mountains. They are raised up
and cast down lower than you know.

Where is the bridge taking us?

He asked, Is the road to the bridge long?

I asked, Is the fog dense at the steps of dawn?
For how many years were you like me?
For how long have you been me?

I said, I do not remember.

He said, I do not remember that I remembered
anything but the road.

And he sang,
On the bridge in another land,
the saxophone announces the end of winter.
On the bridge, strangers confess their mistakes,
when no one joins in the song.

I said to him, For how many years
have we urged the dove to fly
to Sidrat al-Muntaha?*
Fly under our window, O dove: fly and fly!

So he said, It is as if I had lost my emotions—
Soon, we will imitate the voices we had when we were little.
We will lisp our *S*'s and *L*'s.
We will slumber like a pair of doves
on a vine that clothes the house.
Soon, life will dominate us axiomatically.
The mountains are as they are, behind their picture in my memory.
The ancient sky is clear of hue and intellect. If memory does not fail me,
the mountains remain as they were, like their image in my mind.
The air, pleasant and clear and radiant remains as it was,
awaiting me…
It remains as it was.

According to Islamic beliefs, *Sidrat al-Muntaha* is a lotus tree that marks the end of the seventh heaven.

I said, My friend,
the long road has rid me of my body.
I do not feel its clay. I do not feel its states.
Whenever I travel, I fly.
My steps are my visions,
my *I* beckons from afar.

If this path of yours is long,
there is work for me in mythology.

Divine hands trained us to carve our names
into the indices of a willow tree;
we were neither clear nor obscure.
But our style in crossing streets from one time to another
provoked speculation:
Who are these who, when they see a palm tree,
stand silent and prostrate themselves on its shadow?
Who are these who, when they laugh, disturb others?

On the bridge into another land, he said to me,
Strangers are known by the disconnected way they gaze in the water,
by their introversion and their hesitant walk.
Natives proceed with direct steps toward a clear goal.
A stranger walks in rounds, bewildered.

He said to me, Every bridge is a meeting point.
On the bridge I enter into what is outside of me,
and surrender my heart to a bee or a swallow.

I said, Not entirely.
On the bridge I walk to what is inside of me.
I train myself to be alert to what concerns it.
Every bridge is cracked—so you are not you as you were a short while ago.
And beings are not memories.

I am two in one,
or I am one split in two.
O bridge, bridge!
Which of the two fragments am I?

We have been walking on the bridge for twenty years,
we have been walking on the bridge twenty meters, there and back.
And I said, There is not much left.
And he said, There is not much left.

And we said together at once, dreaming:

> I'll walk lightly, steps on the wind—
> a bow that fondles the land of the violin.
> I'll hear the pulse of my blood in the pebbles
> and the veins of the place.
>
> I'll rest my head on the carob tree stump—
> it is my mother, even if she disowns me.
> I'll doze a little, and two small birds will carry me
> higher and higher to a star that deported me.
>
> My spirit will wake to a former pain,
> which comes like a letter from a balcony of memory.
> I'll cry out—I am still alive—because
> I feel the arrow piercing my side.
>
> I'll look to the right, toward the jasmine—
> it was there that I learned those early songs of the body.
> I'll look to the left, toward the sea
> where I learned to fish for foam.
>
> I'll lie like an adolescent.
> This milk on my trousers is the dregs
> of a dream that provoked me and is done.

I'll deny that I am copying
the ancient poet's long siesta
between the eyes of the wild deer.

I'll drink from the garden tap a handful of water.
I am as thirsty as water desiring itself.
I'll ask the first to cross the path,
Have you ever seen a ghost like me,
    searching for his yesterday?
I'll carry my house on my shoulder
and walk like a slow tortoise.
I'll hunt an eagle with a broom, and ask,
In what way have I sinned?

I'll search in mythology and archeology
and in every *-ology* for my old name.
One of the goddesses of Canaan will side with me,
then swear with a flash of lightning,
This is my orphan son.

I'll praise a woman who gives birth to a child
in vitro, knowing it is of no resemblance to her.
I'll weep for a man who died when he awoke.

I will take a line of *al-Ma'arri*, and adjust it:
    My body is a scrap of dust,
    O tailor of being, stitch me!
I will write:
    O creator of death, leave me alone for a while!

I'll wake my dead: Sleepers, we are all alike.
Do you still, like us, dream of the Day of Judgment?
I'll collect the ghazals the wind scattered
in Cordoba, and complete *The Ring of the Dove*.

I'll select from my intimate memories
a description of what is suitable:
the scent of crumpled sheets
after lovemaking,
the scent of grass after rain.
I'll see how the face of the rock grows green.

March roses shall burn me in the land where I was first born.
Pomegranate blossoms will conceive of me,
and I will be born from it once more.

I'll depart from yesterday
when I return to its heritage: in memory.
I'll approach tomorrow when I chase a cunning lark.
I'll know that I am late for my appointment.

I'll know that my tomorrow has just passed,
passed as clouds do, without waiting for me.
And I will know that the sky will soon rain on me,
and that I
am crossing the bridge.

Are we now treading the land of the tale?
It may not be as we imagine—
It is neither milk nor honey.
The sky is ashen,
dawn is still an obscure blue.

What is *time* now?
A bridge that is long and short…
A dawn made long and treacherous, as well.
What is *time* now?

The old land dozes behind the tourist castles,
time emigrates to the star
that burned the love-stricken horseman.

You, O Sleepers, who sleep on needles of memory!
Do you not feel the sound
of earthquakes in the gazelle's hoof?

I said to him, Has fever struck you?

His nightmare continued:
O you who sleep, do you hear
the whisper of the Resurrection in a grain of sand?

I said to him, Are you speaking to me
or to yourself?

He said, I reached the end of the dream...
I saw myself as an old man there,
and I saw my heart chasing my dog there—
it was barking.
I saw my bedroom laughing,
Are you still alive?
Come, let me carry the air for you,
and your wooden stick,
inlaid with Moroccan mother-of-pearl!
How should I bring back the beginning, friend?
    Who am I?
    Who am I without a dream and a woman's company?

I said, We visit what remains of life.
Life as it is, let us train ourselves to love the things
we had, to love things that are not ours and ours.
If we look at them together from above,
like snow falling on the mountains,
the mountains may be as they were,
and the fields as they were,
and life, intuitive and communal.

Are we now entering the land of the tale, my friend?
He said to me, I don't want a place to be buried in.
I want a place to live in, and to curse, if I wish.

And he stared at the bridge:
this is the gate of truth.
We can neither enter nor leave.

Nothing is known from its contrary.
The passageways are closed
and the sky is ashen-faced and narrow,
and the hand of dawn pulls up the fatigues
of the woman army officer,
higher and higher.

We have been on the bridge twenty years.
We have eaten canned food for twenty years.
We have dressed in and out of season.
We have listened to new songs, excellently made,
from the troops barracks.
Our children have married exiled princesses
who change their names.
We left our destinies to those
who love losses in the movies.
We read our tracks in the sand.
We were neither obscure nor clear,
    like the picture of a wide yawning dawn.

I said, Does your wound still torment you, friend?
He said, I feel nothing.
My thought has turned my body
into a register of proofs.
Nothing will prove that I am I
except for an open death on the bridge.
I gaze at a rose in the distance
and the charcoal catches fire.

I gaze at my birthplace, farther out,
and the grave expands.

I said, Gently, do not die now.
Life is possible on the bridge.
The metaphor is wide enough:
it is an isthmus between this world and the next,
between exile and a neighboring land.

He said to me, while the hawks hovered above us,
Take my name as a companion,
tell it about me, and live
until the bridge brings you back to life tomorrow.
Do not say: He died or lived in vain.
Say: He looked down on himself from above
and saw himself clothed in a tree.
And was content with the greeting.

If this road is long
there is work for me in mythology.
I was alone on the bridge on that day
after the Messiah withdrew to
a hill in the outskirts of Jericho, before the Resurrection.
I walk, and I cannot go in or out.
I turn like a sunflower.

At night, I am awakened
by the voice of the night watch, a woman soldier
who sings to her lover,
Promise me nothing.
Do not send me a rose from Jericho!

. VII .

EXILE 3

Like a Hand Tattoo in an Ode by an Ancient Arab Poet

I am he.
He walks before me and I follow.
I do not say to him,
Here, here
was something simple for us:
a green stone. A tree. A street,
an adolescent moon, a reality no longer real.
He walks before me.
I follow his shadow.
As he hurries, his shadow rises over the hills
and covers a pine tree in the South,
and covers a willow tree in the North.

I said: Did we not part?
He said: Yes.
  I owe you the return of fantasy to the real,
  and you owe me the apple's surrender to gravity
I said: Where are you taking me?
He said: Toward the beginning, where you were born.
  Here, you and your name.

If I could return to the beginning,
I would select fewer letters for my name,
letters easier on the foreign ear.

March is a month of storms and lust.
Spring looks on, like a thought between two people,
between a long winter and a long summer.
I remember nothing but allegory.
I was scarcely born when I woke
to a clear image between the horse's mane,
and my mother's braids.
Give up metaphor, and walk quietly
on the earth's down, he said.

Sunset brings the stranger back
to his well, like a song that is not sung.
Sunset stirs up in us a longing for an obscure passion.

Perhaps, perhaps.
Things acquire new meanings at sunset.
Memories wake and call,
like a signal of death at sunset,
like the beat of a song not sung to anyone.

(On the cypress tree,
east of emotions,
gilded clouds,
in the heart, a chestnut brown
transparency of shadows, drunk like water.
Come, let us play;
come, let us go
    to any star.)

I am he. He walks over me
and I ask him,
Do you remember anything here?
Tread softly—remember,
the earth is pregnant with us.

He said: I saw the moon shining here,
    its grief plain, like an orange in the night.
    It guides us in the wilderness to stray paths...
    Without it, mothers could not meet their children.
    Without it, wanderers could not read
    their names in the night: Refugees,
    guests of the wind.

My wings felt small in the wind that year.
I always thought the place was identified
by the mothers and the aroma of sage.

No one said to me,
    this place is called a country,
    around the country are borders,
    and beyond the borders is another place,
    called *diaspora* and *exile* for us.

I did not yet need an identity,
but they, men who came to us on tanks,
are carrying off our place on trucks.

The place is a feeling.
Those are our remains, like hand tattoos
in the *mu'allaqa* of the ancient poet.
They pass us and we pass them.

Thus said the one I was the day I did not know
the details of the names of our trees or the names
the birds who gather in me.
I did not remember the words to defend the place
from its removal, from its strange, new name
hedged with eucalyptus.

The signs say to us,
You were not here.

The storm abates.
The place is a feeling.
Those are our tracks, said he who was I,
Here our two orders of time meet and part.
Who are you in the presence of *now*?

I said: I am you, were it not for the smoke of factories.
He said: Who are you in the presence of yesterday?
I said: I am we, were it not
    for the intrusion of
    a verb in the imperfect tense.

He said: And who will you be tomorrow?
I said: A love poem that you will write when
 you choose—since you are, yourself, a legend of love.

(Golden as old harvest songs,
dark from the sting of the night,
white from the water's endless laughter,
as you approach the spring
your eyes are almonds,
your lips two wounds of honey,
your legs towers of marble,
your hands on my shoulders two birds.
You give me a spirit that flutters
around the place.)

Leave metaphor, and walk with me.
Do you see traces of the moth in the light?

I said: I see you there; I see you pass
 like one of the thoughts of our ancestors.
He said: Thus the moth recalls its poetic labor:
 a song that the astronomers recognize
 as proof of eternity.

I walk slowly by myself
and my shadow follows me, and I, it.
Nothing brings me back.
Nothing brings it back.
As if a part of me were departing,
anxious for tomorrow.
Do not wait for anyone.
Do not wait for me.

But I do not leave him.

As if it were poetry: over the hill,
a cloud deceives me, weaving its identity around,
and bequeaths me an orbit that I will not lose.

This place has its scents.
The sunsets have their torments.
The gazelle has its hunter.
Tortoises have their armor.
Ants have their kingdom.
Birds have their appointments.
Horses have their names.
Wheat flowers have a festival.

But the song, the song of the happy ending,
has not found a poet.

In the last watch of life, we listen
to all sounds, inattentive.
Pain in the joints wakes us from our sleep.
Or a mosquito, droning like a professor of philosophy…

In the last watch,
we feel the pain of amputated legs,
as if the sensation is delayed.
We do not wake when young
to our inner wound.
It, like an oil painting, contains
a fire that burns the colors of our flags,
that stirs the violence of our anthems.

In the last watch of life,
the dawn only breaks
because good angels do their duty, humbly.

I am he, a horseman of myself,
and no horse neighs in my language.

He said: We walk even in the last watch of life.
    We walk though paths have forsaken us.
    We fly like Sufis;
    in words, we fly to any end.

We have ascended a hill as high
as two hands stretched to the sky.
We walk on thorns, on oak.
We wrap ourselves in the orphaned wool of plants,
united with the dictionary of our names.
Do you feel the gravel burning?
    And the cunning of the sand grouse?

He said: I feel nothing, as if sensations were a luxury.
    As if I were here as one of the many properties of absence.
    My life is not with me... It has left me as
    a woman leaves a man—the ghost.
    She waited for me, and wearied of waiting, and
    directed another to her woman's treasure.

    If there is no avoiding a moon then
    let it be a full one, a full one,
    not a horned moon, like a banana.

I said: You need time to know yourself.
    Sit down in the gap of betwixt and between,
    not how how or where where.

On two heavenly rocks we awaited the sunset.
At sunset, the stranger feels the need
to embrace another stranger.
At sunset, two strangers feel that there is,
between them, a third who interrupts
what they are saying or not saying.

Say farewell to what was.
Say farewell to what will be.
Farewell to the rhyme in nun*
in the name of doubles
and in the country of amethyst.

I say: Who is he?

An echo from afar says: This is reality,
the voice of our destinies,
the bulldozer driver who flattened
the spontaneity of this place,
cut the curls of our olive trees
to match an army haircut,
opened a gap for an old prophet's mule.
This is reality, the tamer of legend.
The third of those sitting on two heavenly rocks.
But he does not see us as we are:
an old man with a child under his arm,
and a child tangled in the old man's wisdom.

We said: Greetings to the men and *jinn* around us.
He said: I do not understand the metaphor.
We said: Why do you dive into what we say and feel?
He said: The way your shadow wears the gravel
    and the sand grouse frightens me.
We asked: What are you afraid of?
And he said: The shadow.
    The shadow smells of garlic sometimes,
    and of blood, sometimes.
We asked: Where do you come from?
And he said: From the places.
    Thus every place far from God and His earth is an exile.
    What of yourselves?
And we said: We are the grandsons of the spirit of this place.

nun: the Arabic letter "N"

We were born here, and here we will live
if the Lord is still alive. And every place far from God
and His Earth is an exile.
And he said: The way your shadow wears this place
stirs doubts in me.
And we asked: What do you have doubts about?
And he said: A shadow that fights with another shadow.
And we said: Is it because the space between yesterday
and our present fertilizes the trilogy of time?
He said: I killed you yesterday.
We said: Death granted us amnesty.
He shouted: I am the guard of eternity!
Say farewell to what will be and what was.
Say farewell to the smell of garlic
and blood in the shadow of this place.

Does the thing have meaning when the thing makes me?
He who restores to meaning its features?
How come I am born from a thing… a thing I make?

I am stretched out in a lofty tree. It raises me to the sky,
and I rise as a cautious bird
betrayed by nothing, brought down by nothing.

I see my spirit in everything. I am pained
by what I do not feel, or by what does not sense
my soul when it is in pain.

I and myself—we do not trust this dusty road, yet I follow the ant.
(Appearance is the map of intuition.)
For the sun has not quite set, nor the orange moon given light.

I and myself—we do not believe
that the beginning awaits those who return to it,
like a mother on a doorstep.
We travel, though heaven has forsaken us.

I and myself—we do not believe that the tale
has brought us back to witness what we have done.
I forgot you, like my mulberry-stained shirt,
when you rushed into the woods and repented...
I forgot you while you kept
a phoenix feather for me... and repented.

I said: Are we making peace?
And he said: You better wait. My school is two meters away.
    Come, let us rid the consonants from the spider,
    leave only its weeping vowels!

I remember two ancient walls without a roof,
like two letters of a language that the sands have defaced.
I remember an earthquake, like that of Sodom.

Fat cows sleep on the alphabet; a pleased dog wags its tail.
A short night arranges its affairs to the joys of foxes.

He said: Life continues its routine after us.
    O, how licentious it is. It thinks of nothing
    but the satisfaction of its desire.
I said: Are we making peace so that we may share this
    absence? Are we alone here in this poem?
He said: Over there, on the edge of the hill,
    on the eastern side, lies the graveyard of my people.
    So let us go, before nightfall, to the dead
    and greet those who sleep,
    greet those who dream,
    safe in the garden of Paradise.
    Greet those who lightly mount God's ladder.

In the presence of death,
we cling only to our names.

It is shameless absurdity! Not one stone there bears the name of the victim,
neither my name nor yours.

I asked: Which of us died, I or I?
He said: I do not know now.
I asked: Are we making peace?
He said: You better wait!
And I asked: Is this the desired return?
And he said: And one comedy is our goddess playing.
Does this visit appeal to you?
I asked: Is that the end of your exile?
He said: That is the beginning of your exile.
I asked: And what is the difference?
He said: The cunning of the rhetoric.
I said: Rhetoric is not necessary to justify loss.
He said: Yes, rhetoric persuades a widow
to marry a foreign tourist, and protects
the roses of the garden from the wind's sport.
I said: Are we not making peace?
He said: If a live man and a dead man
sign a truce in one body.
I said: Here am I, both dead and alive.
He said: I have forgotten you... Who are you?
I said: I am a copy of your *I*, who becomes aware
of what the moth said to me: O, my brother in frailty!
He said: But she was burned.
I said: Don't get burned like her.

I turned to him, but could not see him.
I cried out with all my might:
Wait for me!
Take everything, but the name!

He did not wait for me.
He flew and night caught up with me.

My cry attracted a passing ghost.
I said: Who are you?
He said: *Salaam*.
I said: *Salaam* to you. Who are you?
He said: I am a tourist.
    I am fond of your legends.
    And I want to marry a widow
    from among the daughters of Enat!*

Enat: Canaanite goddess of fertility, war, and marriage

. VIII .

EXILE 4

Counterpoint
(For Edward W. Said)

New York. November. Fifth Avenue.
The sun is a plate of scattered metal.
I say to my strange self in the shade,
Is this Babylon or Sodom?

There, at the door of a skyscraper, high in the sky,
I met Edward, thirty years ago.
The time was less willful than now.
We both said: If your past is experience,
    make tomorrow into meaning and vision!
    Let us go, let us go to our tomorrow confidently,
    with the truth of imagination and the miracle of grass.

I do not remember whether we went to the movies
in the evening, but I heard old Indians calling to me,
Trust neither the horse nor modernity!

No victim asks his executioner,
    Am I you?
    If my sword were bigger than my rose,
    Would you ask me if I'd do the same to you?

A question like that arouses the novelist's curiosity,
in his glass office, overlooking lilacs in the garden,
where the hands of hypothesis grow white
like the conscience of the novelist
once he clears his account
with human nature:
No tomorrow in yesterday. Let's go forward.

But going forward might be the bridge of return to barbarism.

New York. Edward wakes to an idle dawn.
He plays Mozart. He runs around the university tennis court.
He thinks about birds migrating across frontiers, and over barriers.
He reads the *New York Times*.
He writes his firm comments.
He curses the Orientalist who guides the general
to the point of weakness in an Oriental heart.
He takes a shower.
He chooses his suit with the elegance of a cockerel.
He drinks milky coffee, and calls to the dawn,
    Come on, don't dawdle.

On the wind, he walks,
and in the wind, he knows who he is.
The wind has no roof; the wind has no house,
the wind is a compass pointing to the stranger's North.

He says: I am from there. I am from here.
    I am not there and I am not here.
    I have two names, which meet and part,
    and I have two languages.
    I forget which of them I dream in.
    I have English for writing, obedient in words.
    I have also a language
    in which heaven speaks to Jerusalem:
    silver-stressed, and it does not obey!

I said: And identity?

He said: Defense of the person. Identity is the daughter of birth,
    but in the end, the invention of its owner,
    not an heirloom from the past.
I am manifold. But I belong to the question
    of the victim. If I were not from there I would train
    my heart to nurture the gazelle of metonymy.
So carry your home country wherever you go,
    and be a narcissist if occasion demands.

Exile is the outside world.
Exile is the inner world.
Who are you between them?
I do not quite identify myself, lest I ruin it.
I am in a duality, which sings something between words and gesture.
If I wrote poetry I would say,

I am two in one,
like the wings of a swallow.
If spring is late,
I am content to be the bearer of good news.

He loves a country, and travels from it.
(Is the impossible far off?)
He loves traveling to anything,
and in free travel between cultures,
those who study human essence
may find space enough for all.

There is a margin that advances,
or a center that recedes.
The East is not entirely East,
and the West not entirely West,
because identity can be multiple,
either a fortress or trenches.

Metaphor was sleeping on the bank of the river.
Had it not been for the pollution,
it would have embraced the other bank.

—Have you written a novel?
I tried... I tried to bring back
my image in the looking-glass
of distant women, but they burrowed into their secure night
and said,
We have a world independent of the text.
No man will write Woman, the riddle and the dream.

No woman will write Man, the symbol and the star.
No night is like another night.
Let us count the qualities of men, and laugh!

—And what did you do?
I laughed at my absurdity,
    and I threw the novel in the wastebasket!

The thinker restrains the flow of the narrative.
    The philosopher dissects the singer's rose.

He loves a country and travels from it:
    I am what I am and what I will be.
    I will make myself by myself,
    and I will choose my exile.
    My exile is the milieu of the heroic spectacle.
    I defend the need of poets for a tomorrow
    and for memories at the same time;
    I defend the tree that birds clothe,
    as a country and a place of exile;
    I defend a moon that is still suitable for a love poem;
    I defend an idea shattered by the frailty of its holders,
    and I defend a country hijacked by legends.

Can you go back to anything?
What is in front of me drags
    what is behind me, and hurries...
I have no time to draw lines in the sand.
    But I can visit yesterday, as strangers do,
    when they listen in the evening
    to the pastoral poet:

(A girl at the spring fills her pitcher
    with the milk of the clouds,
    and she weeps and laughs at a bee
    that has stung her heart in the throes of absence.

Is it love that gives pain to the water
or sickness in the mist?
And so on...)

—So, the sickness of longing afflicts you?
A longing for tomorrow...
further, higher, and further.
My dream leads my steps, my vision
makes my dream sit in my lap
like a domestic cat.
It is a realist and an idealist,
and a son of will:

We can
change
the inevitability of the abyss.

—And the longing for tomorrow?
An emotion that concerns not the thinker,
except to understand the longing of the stranger
for the tools of absence.

But as for me,
my longing is a struggle against a present
that holds tomorrow by the balls.

Did you not infiltrate yesterday
when you went to the house, your house,
in the *Talibiya* quarter?

I prepared myself
so as to stretch out in my mother's bed,
as a child when he fears his father.

I tried to bring back my childhood,
to follow the path of the Milky Way

on the roof-garden of my old house,
and I tried to feel the skin of absence,
and the scent of summer from the jasmine of the garden,
but the desolation of the truth
drove me away from my tortured nostalgia.
I glanced around like a thief.

—Were you afraid?
    What frightened you?
        What frightened you?
I cannot meet loss face to face.
I stood at the door like a beggar.
Should I ask permission from strangers
sleeping in my own bed,
to visit myself for five minutes?
Should I bow respectfully
to the inhabitants of my childish dream?
Would they ask, Who is this inquisitive foreign visitor?
Would I be able to speak
    of peace and war among victims,
    and victims of victims?
Without contradiction? Would they say to me,
There is no room for two dreams in one bedroom?

(Not I or he. The reader will wonder what poetry
    says to us in time of disaster.)

Blood
    and blood
        and blood
            in your land.

In my name and in your name
in the almond blossoms
in the light and shade
in the children's milk

in the grain of wheat
in the tin of salt,
skillful hunters hit the targets
with distinction.

Blood
      and blood
            and blood.

This land is too small for the blood of its children,
who stand on the threshold
of the Resurrection in masses.

Is this land really blessed or baptized
      in blood
            and blood
                        and blood,
which neither prayer nor sand dries.

There is not enough justice
in the pages of the holy book
to rejoice martyrs as they walk free above the clouds.

Blood by day,
      blood in the dark,
            blood in words.

He says: The poem may host loss,
      as a thread of light flashing in the heart of a guitar
      or a Messiah on a horse, pierced by beautiful, figurative language.
      The aesthetic is only
      the incarnation of Truth in form.

      In a world that has no heaven the earth becomes an abyss.
      And the poem is one of its consolation prizes,
      one of the qualities of the winds, North or South.

Do not describe what the camera sees of your wounds.
Shout so that you hear yourself, shout so that you know
that you are still alive, and you know that life is possible on this earth.

Invent a hope for words, or an area, or a mirage,
to prolong hope.
And sing, for beauty is freedom.

I say: Life defined only as the opposite of death is not life.
He says: We shall live,
even if life leaves us to our own devices.
Let us be masters of words
that will make our readers immortal,
as your brilliant friend Ritsos has it.

And he said: And if I die before you
I urge you not to forget the impossible!
I asked: Is the impossible far away?
And he said: A generation away.

I asked: And if I die before you?
He said: I will pay condolences to the mountains of Galilee.
And I will write, *Beauty is only the achieving of what is appropriate.*
And now do not forget—
if I die before you, I leave you the impossible.

When I visited him in New Sodom,
in the year two thousand and two, he was resisting
the war of Sodom against Babylon,
and cancer at the same time.
He was the last hero in that epic,
defending the rights of Troy.

An eagle bids farewell to its peak, rising,
rising,
living above Olympus
    and the peaks
    may bring on boredom.

Farewell.
Farewell to the poetry of pain!